INVESTING

Dennis Brindell Fradin & Judith Bloom Fradin

MONEY SMART

INVESTING

Dennis Brindell Fradin & Judith Bloom Fradin

Marshall Cavendish
Benchmark
New York

Website: www.marshallcavendish.us

This publication represents the opinions and views of the author based on Dennis Brindell Fradin's and
Judith Bloom Fradin's personal experience, knowledge, and research. The information in this book serves
as a general guide only. The author and publisher have used their best efforts in preparing this book
and disclaim liability rising directly and indirectly from the use and application of this book.

Other Marshall Cavendish Offices:
Marshall Cavendish International (Asia) Private Limited, 1 New Industrial Road, Singapore 536196 • Marshall
Cavendish International (Thailand) Co Ltd. 253 Asoke, 12th Flr, Sukhumvit 21 Road, Klongtoey Nua, Wattana,
Bangkok 10110, Thailand • Marshall Cavendish (Malaysia) Sdn Bhd, Times Subang, Lot 46, Subang Hi-Tech
Industrial Park, Batu Tiga, 40000 Shah Alam, Selangor Darul Ehsan, Malaysia

Marshall Cavendish is a trademark of Times Publishing Limited

All websites were available and accurate when this book was sent to press.

Library of Congress Cataloging-in-Publication Data
Fradin, Dennis B.
Investing / Dennis Brindell Fradin and Judith Bloom Fradin.
p. cm. — (Money smart)
Includes bibliographical references and index.
Summary: "Answers basic questions students ask when learning about
financial skills needed for adulthood, including investing money in the
stock market, bonds and mutual funds, gold, and collectibles"—Provided by
publisher.
ISBN 978-1-60870-124-7
1. Finance, Personal—Juvenile literature. 2. Investments—Juvenile
literature. I. Fradin, Judith Bloom. II. Title.
HG179.F6864 2010
332.6—dc22
                                        2010001804

Editor: Deborah Grahame
Publisher: Michelle Bisson
Art Director: Anahid Hamparian
Series Designer: Kay Petronio
Photo research by Connie Gardner

Cover photo by: Bill/Aron/PhotoEdit

The photographs in this book are used by permission and through the courtesy of: *Corbis:* Gareth Brown,
19; Najlah Feanny, 36; *AP Photo;* 6; *Getty Images:* Stephen Wilkes, 12; Taxi, 16; Yellow Dog Productions,
17; Stone, 22; Upper Cut Images, 24; White Packet, 26; Doug Armand, 28; Stephen Chernin,
29; Hulton Archive, 33, 39; Billy Hustace, 40; Justin Sullivan, 43; Jack Vearey, 47; Getty Images,
49; John Moore, 52; *Alamy;* Ian Butterfield, 44.

Printed in Malaysia (T)

135642

CONTENTS

Researchers and inventors often make money for their investors by coming up with odd or unique products.

ONE

INVIS-ALL: A SCIENCE-FICTION TALE ABOUT INVESTING

One summer day in the year 2021, middle school science teacher Delmore Greengrass of Granite Head, New Hampshire, made an astounding discovery while tinkering in his home laboratory. Greengrass was pouring chemicals on some odd-looking reddish dirt he had dug up from his pasture. He accidentally spilled the mixture on his hand, which turned invisible. His hand remained invisible for several minutes before suddenly reappearing.

Amazed by what he had done, Greengrass began a series of experiments. He soon concluded that pouring the mixture on anything made it invisible. A loaf of bread, his wife Wilma's pet parakeet, his car, and even his home would vanish from sight for about eight minutes. The object would then reappear.

Greengrass named his wondrous potion Invis-All. At first, Greengrass gave little thought to making money from it. Invis-All made its public debut on Halloween of 2021, when Delmore and Wilma covered their granddaughter Sarah with the potion before she began trick-or-treating. When neighbors answered their doorbells, they heard Sarah's disembodied voice say, "I'm the Invisible Girl. Trick or treat!"

Word about Invis-All spread quickly, and in November Greengrass was invited to demonstrate his discovery on *UnReality*, a popular TV show. Before tens of millions of viewers, he made a beagle puppy, a birthday cake, and the show's host disappear from sight.

After the *UnReality* broadcast, Greengrass was flooded with requests for Invis-All. He rented an old factory and put half the population of Granite Head to work mixing, bottling, and shipping batches of Invis-All to customers. Soon Greengrass was making his own TV ads for his Invis-All Company (IAC), and he was on the road to wealth.

In early 2022, Greengrass hit it big. The U.S. military ordered a gigantic quantity of Invis-All. Invisible planes, tanks, and soldiers would be a great advantage in wartime.

Producing vast amounts of Invis-All for the military was too big a job for Greengrass and his fifty employees. Greengrass decided it was time for IAC to "go public." He gave up being IAC's sole owner and divided ownership of the company into a number of shares,

IF IT SOUNDS TOO GOOD TO BE TRUE...

It is important to beware of fake investment offers. There are many true stories about crooks trying to sell people shares of stock in fake oil wells or useless products. If it sounds too good to be true, it probably is. So be wary if someone named Delmore Greengrass asks you to invest in a business that makes an invisibility potion.

which would be sold and bought on the stock market. The people who bought shares in IAC would own the company jointly.

At first, everyone gained from IAC's success. Greengrass made a fortune in the deal that placed the firm on the stock market. As the growing company filled orders for the potion, Invis-All stock doubled, tripled, and then quadrupled in value. At one point investors who had bought $5,000 of IAC stock could sell it for $100,000. But then the problems started.

Some objects lost the ability to reappear. Tanks and airplanes that had been sprayed with Invis-All repeatedly simply stayed invisible. Worse still, thousands of people seemed doomed to remain invisible for the rest of their lives. Buried beneath a mountain of lawsuits and debts, IAC went out of business, and its stock became completely worthless. News headlines proclaimed, INVIS-ALL COMPANY DISAPPEARS!

The fate of IAC's investors depended on when they bought and sold—or didn't sell—their shares. People lost large sums of money if they had bought shares soon after IAC went on the stock market and held on to them until the company went out of business. People became wealthy if they had invested in IAC at the start and then sold their stock when its price soared.

Of course this is a fictitious story. There is no invisibility potion or Invis-All Company. Yet, as you will see, purchasers of stocks and other investments are making and losing money constantly in today's economy.

The size of an average U.S. household today is about half what it was a century ago.

TWO

INVESTING: WHAT IS IT AND WHY DO IT?

As of 2010, there were about 300 million people living in about 100 million separate households in the United States. Some households had four, five, or even eight or more people. Other households consisted of just one or two people. The average household contained three people—in many cases a mother, a father, and a child.

In the same year, about one out of every twenty-five households had a yearly income of $200,000 or more. These were the nation's wealthiest people. On the other hand, one out of every five households earned less than $20,000 annually. This large segment of the population comprised the poorest Americans. But the average household income in the United States was about $60,000.

WHAT IS HOUSEHOLD INCOME?

Household income is the combined yearly income of all the adult members of a household. The people in the household do not have to be related. As an example, let's imagine a five-person household composed of a father, a mother, two young children, and a grown cousin. The father, a newspaper reporter, earned $35,000 for the year, while the mother, a musician, made $25,000. The couple also earned $5,500 from investments. The cousin earned $40,000 as an auto mechanic. Thus, this family's household income was $35,000 + $25,000 + $5,500 + $40,000 = $105,500.

Sixty thousand dollars might sound like a ton of money, but life's basic expenses can easily gobble up $60,000 in a year. To begin with, a typical new house sells for about $250,000 dollars. Few families can afford to pay that much money at once. Most people pay for their homes gradually by making monthly mortgage payments. Average mortgage payments are about $1,200 per month, or $14,400 per year. That eats up almost a quarter of a typical family's $60,000 income! People who rent apartments have to spend roughly the same amount of money each year.

Paying for a place to live is the single largest expense for most families. It is hardly the only major expense, however. People need to get from place to place. Most families buy a car every few years. In 2010, the average cost of a new car was $29,000. A good used car might cost half that much. Either way, there goes another large slice of a family's annual income.

And don't forget—everyone has to eat. Not counting people who grow their own fruits and vegetables, the typical American family spends about $2,500 per person on food each year. That means a family of four spends a whopping $10,000 for groceries annually.

Everyone wears clothes, too. Clothing a baby for the first year typically totals nearly $1,000—and that doesn't include the cost of diapers. Even if they aren't very fashion-conscious, a family of four can easily spend two or three thousand dollars a year on clothes and shoes.

The list of expenses goes on and on. Electricity, water, natural gas, and telephone service are known as utilities. The average household pays between three and four thousand dollars per year on utilities.

After housing costs, groceries are the most significant expense for families.

In 1789 Benjamin Franklin wrote, "In this world nothing can be said to be certain, except death and taxes." Franklin would be shocked by all the taxes Americans pay today. Federal income tax takes the largest tax bite out of most Americans' paychecks. Most U.S. states also have state income taxes. Then there are property taxes and various other local, state, and federal taxes. Put them all together, and what have you got? One-third of the typical American family's income is spent on taxes—roughly $20,000 for a household with an annual income of $60,000. Tax money pays for schools, the armed services, highways and bridges, national parks, and thousands of government services.

Health care is a huge expense for millions of American households. A family can spend thousands of dollars a year on doctor and hospital visits, prescriptions, braces, and eyeglasses. Insurance bills can also be colossal. Taken together, health, homeowners, life, and automobile insurance can eat up thousands of dollars per year.

People pay taxes to fund highway construction projects like this one.

WHAT IS INSURANCE?

Insurance protects people against various kinds of financial disaster. Customers pay a certain amount for insurance per year—perhaps $5,000 for health insurance and $2,000 for auto insurance. If they become ill and are hospitalized, their health insurance pays many of the costs. If insured people get into car accidents, their auto insurance pays the bulk of the bills. Even though insurance companies sometimes pay out huge sums of money to their customers, they make healthy profits. That is because in a given year, relatively few insured customers have to use their insurance because of an illness or accident.

Imagine what happens when a family decides to take a vacation! It doesn't come free. Depending on where they go and for how long, a family can spend anywhere from a few hundred to thousands of dollars on a getaway. Even a weekly family night out for dinner can be costly. By spending $40 a week at restaurants, a family will part with more than $2,000 over the course of a year.

Despite all these bills, many Americans try to set aside a portion of their paychecks. Parents save money for their children's college education, which can be very pricey. Although Social Security provides income for elderly people, senior citizens need a lot of additional money in order to live well. That means adults need a retirement fund starting early in their careers. It is also wise to set aside money for hard times, such as periods of unemployment or illness. This is commonly called saving for a "rainy day."

How can an average family stretch out $60,000 for house payments, taxes, a car, and all their other expenses? Generally speaking, they can't. Most people need more money to pay their bills and to save for college, retirement, and a rainy day. And even if they don't *need* it,

Working adults who want an active retirement with few financial worries must save money wisely.

THE HIGH COST OF COLLEGE

Going to college in the United States has become extremely expensive. Four years at a public college or university can cost $80,000 or more, including tuition, housing, food, and other expenses. Four years at a private college or university can run $150,000 or more. It is very difficult to pay for college on a $60,000-a-year income. That is why many families rely on a combination of scholarships, loans, and investments to pay for their kids' college education.

most people would *like* to have more money. That's where investing comes in.

Investing is similar to saving, but it is different in key ways. People typically save money by using banks. For the right to hold and temporarily use your money, banks pay savers a fee called interest. In 2010, most banks paid a low interest rate—sometimes less than one percent. That means if you had $10,000 in a bank account that paid 2 percent in annual interest, you would receive $200 in interest for the year.

Why do people save money in banks if they pay such little interest? Banks keep your money safe. People who put their money in bank accounts know that their money will be there when they want it. Now and then a bank does go out of business. In that case, however, the

U.S. government usually steps in and replaces the customers' money. Investors, on the other hand, take risks with their money. They buy

HOW DO BANKS MAKE MONEY?

Have you ever wondered how banks make a profit? Banks pay small amounts of interest to people who have savings accounts with them. At the same time, they charge much higher interest to people who take out house mortgages and other loans. The difference between these amounts of interest is profit for the banks. Banks also make profits by investing some of their money and by charging fees for their services.

shares in the stock market or take part in risky business ventures. Investors take the chance that they will lose part—or all—of their money. For some investors, this is exactly what happens. But it is also possible for investors to make a lot of money—way more than they would make from interest in a bank account. Between 1971 and 2001, stock market investors averaged 11 percent in yearly earnings. Thus, a $10,000 investment in stocks typically earned $1,100 in just the first year. That's why millions of Americans put their money in stocks.

There is another reason that people are willing to risk their money by investing. That reason is a money-eating monster called inflation.

As a result of inflation, food prices today are higher than any time since just after World War II.

THREE

INFLATION: ANOTHER REASON TO INVEST

Over time, the cost of almost everything grows like a balloon being blown up. This gradual increase in prices is known as inflation. Due to inflation, the value of the dollar steadily shrinks because it takes more dollars to pay for goods and services.

For example, in the twenty-five years between 1985 and 2010, the cost of living doubled. This doesn't mean that everything in 2010 was exactly twice as expensive as it was in 1985. Some items were four times as expensive, while other prices had hardly changed. Taken all together, though, the cost of housing, groceries, transportation, and other goods and services doubled.

What if someone who earned $40,000 a year in 1985 still made $40,000 in 2010? Based on the numbers, the person's salary did not

Shopping with coupons can help people with fixed or low incomes, such as students, save some money on groceries.

change. In terms of buying power, though, a salary of $40,000 in 2010 would be worth just half of what it was in 1985. To have the same buying power in 2010 that the worker had in 1985, he or she would have to earn $80,000.

Inflation has devoured Americans' incomes for as long as records have been kept. Many items that cost $50 in 1960 cost more than $350 in 2010. This means you will pay more than seven times what your grandparents paid for the same items a half century ago. It is especially startling to see how housing costs have increased throughout American history. For instance, Abraham Lincoln and his wife Mary bought a nice house in Springfield, Illinois, for $1,200 in 1844. These days a similar home would cost roughly a hundred times that much.

Inflation is still nibbling away at people's buying power. As inflation eats up more and more dollars, what can we do? For millions of Americans, the answer is . . . invest!

Stock certificates are legal documents that certify ownership of shares in a corporation. Some older ones are collected as works of art.

THE STOCK MARKET

You may have heard people say that they "invest in stocks" or "play the stock market." Stocks are shares of ownership in companies. People who buy and sell stocks are called investors. The term *stock market* refers to the entire system by which shares are traded. Places where a large amount of trading is done are called stock exchanges.

The city of Philadelphia has the country's oldest stock exchange. The Philadelphia Stock Exchange was founded in 1790, just fourteen years after the Declaration of Independence gave birth to the United States. The world's largest stock exchange was founded in New York City in 1817. The New York Stock Exchange is located on Wall Street in the biggest U.S. city. People often use the term *Wall Street* to refer to the entire American stock trading industry. This is because, in addition to the New York Stock Exchange, many banks and financial businesses are located in the Wall Street area.

A view of the New York Stock Exchange on Wall Street. For security reasons, it is no longer open for tours.

The NASDAQ market site is located in Times Square, New York City.

The nation's newest major stock exchange, founded in 1971, is called the NASDAQ. It is not a physical place. Instead, the NASDAQ consists of a computer network.

Stocks of many well-known companies are bought and sold in the stock market. Some familiar names are Coca-Cola, PepsiCo, McDonald's, Wal-Mart, Kellogg, General Mills, Kraft Foods, Microsoft, Dell, Mattel, Toys "R" Us, and Walt Disney Company.

Companies sell their stocks to raise money. Then they use the funds to improve old products and to create new ones, to hire more workers, and to modernize equipment and buildings. Investors buy and sell stocks to make a profit. Experts called stockbrokers advise many investors about which stocks to buy and when to buy or sell them. Investors pay stockbrokers a fee to handle the buying and selling of stocks. In recent years, however, many investors have been making their own trades through Internet-based investment firms.

When investors buy a company's stock, they actually own a piece of that company. The price of a share of stock is expressed in dollars. For example, a stock might be selling for $100 a share. Over days, weeks, months, and years, the cost of a share of stock changes. The stock of a profitable company will tend to rise in value. For example, the price of one share might jump from $100 to $120, $150, or more. On the other hand, if a company struggles and loses money, its stock will tend to drop in value. It might fall from $100 to $80, $50, or less.

DIVIDENDS

When a company makes a profit, it may distribute a portion of the money to its stockholders. These payments are called dividends, and they can be a pleasant bonus for owning stocks.

Even the stocks of a successful company can drop in value. Perhaps the firm is not yet well established. Perhaps the stock market as a whole is doing poorly, so stock prices are down overall. But generally speaking, investors look for companies that are on the brink of success and have undervalued stock. The goal is to buy stocks at low prices, to watch them soar in value, and then to sell the stocks at a profit.

The overall health of the stock market is measured in several ways. One is called the Dow Jones Industrial Average. The Dow is a complex formula based on the daily selling prices of stocks of thirty major companies. The Dow is expressed in points. For example, on Monday, September 28, 2009, the Dow began at 9,665 points. It ended the day at 9,789. For that day the Dow was up 124 points—a large gain that provided many investors with a handsome profit. The Dow began the next day at 9,789 and closed at 9,742. For that day the Dow was down 47 points—a small loss that lessened the value of some stocks slightly.

When the stock market has a prolonged "up" period of rising prices, it is known as a bull market. A prolonged "down" period of falling prices is called a bear market. These trends can last months or even years.

Now and then the stock market enjoys huge gains. On October 13,

We do not know for certain how the terms *bull market* and *bear market* came about. Some say that periods of rising stock prices are called bull markets because bulls turn their horns upward when they fight. Periods of falling stock prices might be called bear markets because bears strike with their paws in a downward motion. Others say that the animals' personalities inspired the terms. Bulls are known for being brave and charging ahead. Bears, on the other hand, can be sluggish and cautious.

2008, the Dow Jones Industrial Average climbed 936 points. This was its largest single-day gain ever.

Occasionally the stock market experiences huge losses called crashes. These can occur because of downturns in the nation's economy. Panic about political events or terrorist attacks can also trigger crashes. A memorable crash took place in fall 1929, when the Dow lost half its value. This famous 1929 stock market crash began the Great Depression, a period of hard times and joblessness that lasted for a decade. During the recession of 2007 to 2009, the Dow suffered its greatest one-day point loss ever. On September 29, 2008, the Dow plunged 778 points.

In the wake of the stock market crash of October 1929, people crowded outside the New York Stock Exchange.

For every stock transaction, there is a buyer and a seller. When a buyer and seller agree on the price, a stock trade can be made. The price of a stock tends to rise when it is in demand. This can occur for various reasons, such as an announcement that the company is being purchased by a large corporation. Prices tend to fall when there is little demand for a stock. This can also occur for various reasons, such as a poor earnings report for the company.

Remember that the Dow is a sampling of just thirty stocks. In all, shares of more than six thousand U.S.-based companies are traded on major American stock exchanges. For every firm listed on the Dow, there are two hundred other companies whose stocks are also traded. During the worst crashes, some stocks can increase in value and make their owners rich. The reverse is also true. During good times when fortunes are being made, some investors can lose their savings by buying stocks that decrease in value.

Overall, though, the stock market has risen more than it has fallen. Over decades most investors have made a profit. In fact, stocks have created more wealth for Americans than any other kind of investment has. Between the 1920s and the early twenty-first century, investors in stocks made an average yearly profit of about 10 percent.

Imagine that Wilma Greengrass, Delmore's wife, invested $10,000 in the stock market in 1980. Say her stocks earned 10 percent a year for thirty years, so that her investments were worth $175,000 by 2010. That's seventeen times more money than she had in 1980. Now *that's* a great profit—and a far more reliable investment than Delmore's invisibility potion!

A mutual funds trader analyzes stock performance using multiple flat screens on her company's trading floor.

FIVE

BONDS AND MUTUAL FUNDS

There are many theories about how to strike it rich on the stock market. Not all theories are accurate. Some of them are pretty weird. According to the hemline theory, the direction of the market is linked to women's clothing styles. When women wear long dresses and skirts, the stock market falls. Short dresses and skirts suggest that stocks will skyrocket.

Financial experts do agree on one strategy for investment success. They call it diversification. It means spreading out your money among various kinds of investments. Some investments should be risky, others not so risky. Some should be expensive, others not so expensive. Stocks should come from different types of companies—for example, some in the health industry, others in the entertainment field. Owning a variety of stocks reduces the risk of suffering a big loss from any one investment. In other words, investors should not put all their eggs in one basket.

Investors also diversify by purchasing bonds as well as stocks. Bonds are loans that investors make to companies and governments. In exchange for using your money for a length of time, the business or government agrees to pay you a certain amount of yearly interest. When the bond matures, the principal (original money) is returned to investors. Now they have their original investment back, plus whatever interest they made off the deal.

People buy bonds through stockbrokers and, in some cases, directly from the government. Stocks and bonds differ in that stockholders own a piece of the company in which they invest. Bondholders do not. Another difference is that over time bonds generally earn less money than stocks. Bonds are also less likely than stocks to lose money. Therefore, bonds attract investors who want to minimize risk.

Besides being an investment, buying government bonds is a way to help the nation. For example, the Liberty Bonds of 1917 to 1918 were issued to raise funds for the country's involvement in World War I. They raised about $20 billion for the war effort. New York Liberty Bonds were issued following the terrorist attacks of September 11, 2001. They were sold to pay for rebuilding areas

Boy Scouts promote the sale of Liberty Bonds in New York circa 1918.

of New York City that were damaged or destroyed.

With a type of investment called mutual funds, money from a large number of investors gets pooled together. Financial experts called fund managers determine how that money should be invested. Mutual fund investments are typically a combination of dozens of stocks and/or bonds.

Compared with other investments, mutual funds are very affordable. One share of an individual stock can cost hundreds of dollars. However, for as little as a $100 investment in a mutual fund, people can buy small pieces of many stocks and bonds. For many investors with little money to spare, mutual funds are the only way to diversify.

Land has remained a good investment. More than 60 percent of land in the United States is privately owned.

SIX

REAL ESTATE

"Buy land," advised author Mark Twain. "They're not making it anymore." Millions of Americans have taken Twain's advice by investing in real estate, which refers to land and the buildings on it.

One of the greatest real estate deals in history took place in 1626. In that year, the Dutch bought Manhattan Island in present-day New York City from some American Indians for $24 worth of beads and other trade goods. Today, it can cost that much to park your car for a few hours in Manhattan, and the island and the buildings on it are worth trillions of dollars. The Indians may have had the last laugh, though. Having no concept of owning land, they had made no claim to Manhattan Island!

Back in the early days of the United States, many of the nation's Founding Fathers became wealthy by investing in land. George Washington was one of them. By age sixteen, George was working as a surveyor—someone who figures out land boundaries. With his pay for surveying, young Washington bought land. By the age of nineteen, he owned about 1,500 acres (600 hectares)—more than 2 square miles of land. Eventually Washington owned about 70,000 acres (28,328 ha) in what are now at least seven states. This amounted to more than 100 square miles (260 square kilometers) of land.

Today there are several ways to make money from real estate. Investors still buy land, just as George Washington did. Land often increases in value slowly. However, investors can become rich quickly if builders want to put up homes or shopping malls on their property.

Some investors try to predict which neighborhoods in a city will soon be "hot." They buy an old, run-down home in one of those neighborhoods. Then they spend their spare time fixing it up and sell it at a profit—for example, at a price of $30,000 more than they paid for it. Investors who buy, fix up, and sell two homes a year this way (also called "flipping") can make $60,000.

Apartment buildings are another type of real estate investment. An apartment building's owner is called the landlord. The tenants, or people who live in the building, pay the landlord rent.

The rate of vacant (empty) apartments reached a twenty-two year high during the recession of 2007 to 2009.

If each of twenty tenants pays $1,000 in monthly rent, that amounts to $240,000 in a year. This money doesn't all go into the landlord's pocket, though. Besides purchasing the building, the landlord has to pay property taxes and repair bills. When tenants are in short supply, empty apartments can be costly for landlords. Depending on all these factors, owning an apartment building can provide a profit or a loss. Like any other investment, real estate involves risk.

Tutankhamun's golden coffins are housed in Cairo's Museum of Egyptian Antiquities.

SEVEN

GOLD AND COLLECTIBLES

For thousands of years, people around the world have prized a yellowish metal called gold. The ancient Egyptians buried their kings with this valuable substance. For example, Egyptian king Tutankhamun had a solid gold sarcophagus, or coffin, weighing about 3,000 pounds (1.4 metric tons). About 3,000 years after King Tut's death, the discovery of a large quantity of the gleaming substance set off a "rush" of gold hunters to California.

People value gold because it is rare and beautiful. Along with other metals, gold has been used to make jewelry and coins. Investors like gold because it has risen in value over time. People often invest in gold to protect their money against inflation. The value of gold rises in times of crisis and falls when world events are more stable. Back in 1975, gold sold for $140 an ounce. The price had risen to $353 per ounce in 1990 and just over $1,000 an ounce in January 2010. That made gold seven times as valuable in 2010 as it had been thirty-five years earlier.

Investors sometimes buy gold in the form of bars in various sizes. At 2010 prices, a 10-ounce gold bar would be worth $10,000. A 1-kilogram (2.2-pound) bar would be worth $32,000. A gold bar weighing 12.5 kilograms (27.5 pounds) would be worth $400,000 in 2010 dollars.

WORTH ITS WEIGHT IN GOLD

Gold is weighed according to a special measuring unit called the troy ounce. A troy ounce is a little heavier than the ounce used to weigh a baby or a bag of fruit at the grocery store. That means 6 troy ounces of gold actually weighs a little more than 6 ounces of yogurt.

Bars of gold pose a problem for their owners. Where do you store them safely? Many investors arrange to keep a gold certificate rather than the actual gold bars. The gold itself stays at a bank or other financial institution. Its owner receives a certificate saying that the

Investors who buy gold bars often store them at a bonded vault facility. Gold coins and ingots can be kept in a safety deposit box at a bank.

gold belongs to him or her. If the owner needs money, the gold bars can usually be sold quickly.

Some people combine a hobby with investing. Their investments take the form of collectibles. These are items in various categories, such as coins, stamps, baseball cards, and dolls.

Coin collecting is a way to learn about the history and famous people of different countries. Coins can also be excellent investments, as a large U.S. cent from 1796 shows. Back in the late 1700s, when George Washington and Thomas Jefferson carried pennies like these in their pockets, they were worth exactly what they said: ONE CENT. Not so today! In 2008, a large U.S. cent minted in 1796 sold for $690,000. This was a record high price for a U.S. copper coin sold at auction.

AUCTIONS

An auction is a gathering at which people bid, or offer money, for items. The person who bids the most gets to buy the item. Auctions are held for real estate, rare stamps and coins, paintings and sculptures, antiques, livestock, and other goods and services.

What makes a coin valuable? One factor is the metal it's made of. Gold and silver coins tend to be worth more than copper, nickel, and bronze coins. Age and condition also help determine a coin's worth. The main factor, however, is its rarity. A coin with only twelve known specimens is usually worth more than a coin with a thousand specimens.

Rare coins almost certainly increase in value over time. For example, an old coin book reveals that in 1956 an 1894-S dime was worth $2,500. (The coin was minted in 1894. The "S" stands for where it was minted, San Francisco.) That's quite a sum for a coin originally worth only ten cents. Yet in the past half century, 1894-S dimes have grown in value by leaps and bounds. In 2007 one of them sold for $1.5

The rare 1933 Double Eagle gold coin. Since a $10 gold piece was know as an "eagle," the $20 piece became the "double eagle."

million. In 1956 an 1870-S silver dollar was worth $2,500. In 2007 one of the nine known 1870-S silver dollars sold for $552,000—more than two hundred times the coin's value fifty-one years earlier. One of the world's most valuable coins is the 1933 Double Eagle—the twenty-dollar gold piece once made in the United States. In 2002, one of the few Double Eagles in existence sold for $7.6 million!

How do you obtain valuable coins? You might find them in antique couches and chairs. You might discover them in pockets of old clothes or in attics of old homes. You can buy them at coin shops and auctions and then wait several years as they grow in value. You need not be a big-time collector to invest in coins for fun and profit. By collecting lots of coins that are slightly valuable, you can assemble a collection worth a few thousand dollars.

Stamp collecting can also be a profitable hobby. Old letters are a likely place to find valuable stamps. A twelve-year-old boy discovered one of the world's most valuable stamps in his family's attic in 1873. It was a one-cent stamp issued in 1856 by the South American country of British Guiana, which is called Guyana today. In 1980, this one-of-a-kind stamp was sold at an auction for $935,000.

SUPER DIVERSIFICATION

Some wealthy people have enough money to diversify in a big way. They own stocks, bonds, mutual funds, real estate, gold, and other kinds of investments. Through such extreme diversification, they hope to be able to withstand any downturns in the economy.

As with coins, rare stamps grow in value over time. In fact, few investments are as likely to increase in value as stamps and coins. And if you happened to make a million dollars from a rare one-cent coin or stamp, you could buy your home and send your kids to college with something that originally cost a penny!

Other collectibles can also make good investments. Some people collect dolls or toys from around the world. Baseball cards attract many collectors. Two highly prized baseball cards feature the great ballplayers Honus Wagner and Mickey Mantle. The Honus Wagner card dates from 1909 to 1911. There are only about fifty in existence. In 2007 one of them sold for $2.8 million. The Mickey Mantle rookie card dates from 1952. In excellent condition, one of these cards has sold for as much as $250,000. Some people have valuable baseball cards packed away in shoeboxes in attics and closets and don't even know they are there.

As the economic crisis worsened in 2009, many families were evicted from their homes when they fell behind in their mortgage payments.

EIGHT

A RAINY DAY: THE RECESSION OF 2007 TO 2009

Sometimes nations suffer hard financial times. The stock market crashes and keeps plunging. Businesses fail. Men and women lose their jobs and can't find new ones. Families lose their homes because they can't afford their mortgage payments. If these conditions become extremely bad, the result is called a depression. Today, some elderly people remember the worst depression in the nation's history, the Great Depression of 1929 to 1939. At one point in 1933, 25 percent of American workers were jobless—a gigantic unemployment rate.

When economic conditions are bad but not as terrible as they are during a depression, the result is called a recession. A recession struck the United States in 2007. Two years later, it was still happening. Economists disagree about the causes of this recent recession. However, most of them do agree that the recession was one of the worst economic disasters to strike the nation in years.

Several things went wrong at the same time. The stock market suffered a series of crashes. The Dow Jones Industrial Average fell a record 778 points on September 29, 2008. Many more rough days followed. Between September 2007 and January 2009, the stock market lost nearly $10 trillion. This amounted to 43 percent—nearly half—of its total value. Investments that older people had counted on for their retirement lost about a third of their value. Investments that parents were counting on to send their kids to college also crashed and burned.

Meanwhile, businesses were struggling. Many companies had to close their doors permanently or let some of their employees go. By September 2009, 10 percent of the nation's workers were unemployed. This was the worst jobless rate since 1983, twenty-six years earlier.

The one-two punch of plunging stock prices and joblessness left huge numbers of Americans unable to pay their bills. Millions of homes went into foreclosure because their owners could no longer make their monthly mortgage payments. Millions of families were forced to leave their homes and move in with friends or relatives.

To make things worse, other countries around the world suffered the same economic downturn as the United States. This is because many nations are linked together economically. They trade with each other, borrow money from each other, and lend one another money. Economists called the situation a global recession.

By 2010, there appeared to be good news on the horizon. Economists thought that the crisis was ending and that better times were on their way.

GLOSSARY

antique — Old and valuable.

auction — A gathering at which people bid to buy items.

bear market — A prolonged period of falling stock prices.

bonds — Interest-paying loans made by investors to companies and governments.

bull market — A prolonged period of rising stock prices.

collectibles — Valuable groups of items such as stamps, coins, antique dolls, and baseball cards.

crashes — Events during which the stock market suffers huge losses over a short period of time.

depression — A period of severe joblessness and reduced business activity.

diversification — The strategy of making a variety of investments in order to reduce risk.

dividends — Portions of profits that companies sometimes pay their stockholders.

economists — Experts about money and financial systems.

foreclosure — A process that can result in a lender's seizing a house and forcing its occupants out.

inflation — The increase in the price of goods and services over time.

interest — A charge or fee for the privilege of using funds belonging to another person or business.

investing — The act of risking money in the stock market or another financial venture in the hope of making more money.

investors — People who buy stocks, real estate, or other items of value in the hope of making a profit.

mortgage — A large loan for a home or other item of value.

mutual funds — A type of investment in which money from many people is pooled together to buy numerous stocks and/or bonds.

real estate — Land and the buildings on it.

recession — A period of high unemployment and money shortages resulting from a slump in the economy.

shares — The portions or units of a company's stock.

Social Security — A U.S. government program that provides income for elderly and retired people.

stock — A share in the ownership of a company.

stock exchanges — Places where a great deal of stock trading occurs.

stock market — The entire system by which stocks are traded.

stockbrokers — People who advise investors about which stocks to buy and sell and when to do it.

stockholders — Investors who own shares of ownership in a company.

traded — Bought or sold stocks.

transaction — A deal, especially one involving money.

undervalued — Priced below its true worth.

utilities — Services such as electricity, water, natural gas, and telephone.

BOOKS

Brancato, Robin F. *Money: Getting It, Using It, and Avoiding the Traps: The Ultimate Teen Guide*. Lanham, MD: The Scarecrow Press, 2007.

Deering, Kathryn R., ed. *Cash and Credit Information for Teens: Tips for a Successful Financial Life*. Detroit: Omnigraphics, 2005.

Denega, Danielle. *Smart Money: How to Manage Your Cash*. New York: Franklin Watts, 2008.

Orr, Tamra. *A Kid's Guide to Stock Market Investing*. Hockessin, DE: Mitchell Lane Publishers, 2009.

WEBSITES

For a wealth of information for kids on stocks, bonds, and other forms of investing:

http://library.thinkquest.org/3096/

For an excellent description for kids about various ways to invest, including the stock market:

www.themint.org/kids/what-is-the-stock-market.html

For clear and simple descriptions of investing and finance:

www.wdfi.org/ymm/kids/investing/default.asp

For all kinds of fun facts about money, finance, and investing:

www.factmonster.com/ipka/A0801192.html

BIBLIOGRAPHY

Chatzky, Jean. *Talking Money: Everything You Need to Know About Your Finances and Your Future*. New York: Warner Books, 2001.

Ivey, Allison. *The Geek's Guide to Personal Finance*. Birmingham, AL: Crane Hill Publishers, 2006.

Morris, Kenneth M., and Virginia B. Morris. *The Wall Street Journal Guide to Understanding Money & Investing*. New York: Lightbulb Press, 2004.

Sander, Peter. *The Everything Personal Finance Book: Manage, Budget, Save, and Invest Your Money Wisely*. Avon, MA: Adams Media Corporation, 2003.

Savage, Terry. *The Savage Truth on Money*. New York: John Wiley & Sons, 1999.

Singletary, Michelle. *Spend Well, Live Rich: How to Get What You Want with the Money You Have*. New York: Ballantine, 2004.

Stawski, Willard II. *Kids, Parents & Money: Teaching Personal Finance from Piggy Bank to Prom*. New York: John Wiley & Sons, 2000.

Tucker, Sheryl Hilliard, and the eds. of *Money* magazine, editors. *The New Money Book of Personal Finance*. New York: Warner Books, 2002.

real estate investments and, 43
stocks and, 10, 30–31, 34–35

"rainy day" savings, 19

rarity, collectible coins and,
48–49

rates of return, 20, 21
See also profits and losses
real estate, 41–43

recession of 2007 to 2009, 32,
53–55

rental properties, 42–43

retirement savings, 19, 54

risk, investing and, 21, 37–38,
43

savings, 18–19, 54

share prices, 30, 34

stamp collecting, 50

stockbrokers, 30

stock exchanges, 27–29

stock market crashes, 32

stocks
businesses and, 9–10
depressions and recessions, 53,
54

investing in, 27–35
mutual funds and, 39
rate of return and, 21
stock certificates, **26**

supply and demand, share
prices and, 34

taxes, 16–17

tenants, 42–43

Tutankhamun, sarcophagus of,
44, 45

unemployment, 53, 54

utility costs, 15

Washington, George, 42

wealth creation, stocks and,
34–35

ABOUT THE AUTHORS

Dennis and Judy Fradin are the authors of more than 150 books. They co-author many of their books, but in some cases Dennis writes the text and Judy obtains the pictures. The Fradins first became known for their fifty-two-book series about the states, *From Sea to Shining Sea*, which they did for Children's Press. Their first series for Marshall Cavendish Benchmark was *Turning Points in U.S. History*.

In recent years the Fradins have written many award-winning books about the Underground Railroad, early American history, and great but underappreciated women. Their Clarion book *The Power of One: Daisy Bates and the Little Rock Nine* was named a Golden Kite Honor Book. Another of their Clarion books, *Jane Addams: Champion of Democracy*, won the Society of Midland Authors Best Children's Nonfiction Book of the Year Award.

Currently the Fradins are working on several projects, including a picture book about a slave escape for Walker and a book on *Tornadoes* for National Geographic Children's Books. In addition, Dennis is writing the text and Judy is obtaining the pictures for *Kids Who Overcame*, a book about young people who overcame handicaps to achieve something noteworthy.

The Fradins have three grown children and six grandchildren. In their free time, Judy is a passionate gardener with a special love for dahlias, and Dennis is an amateur astronomer and huge baseball fan.